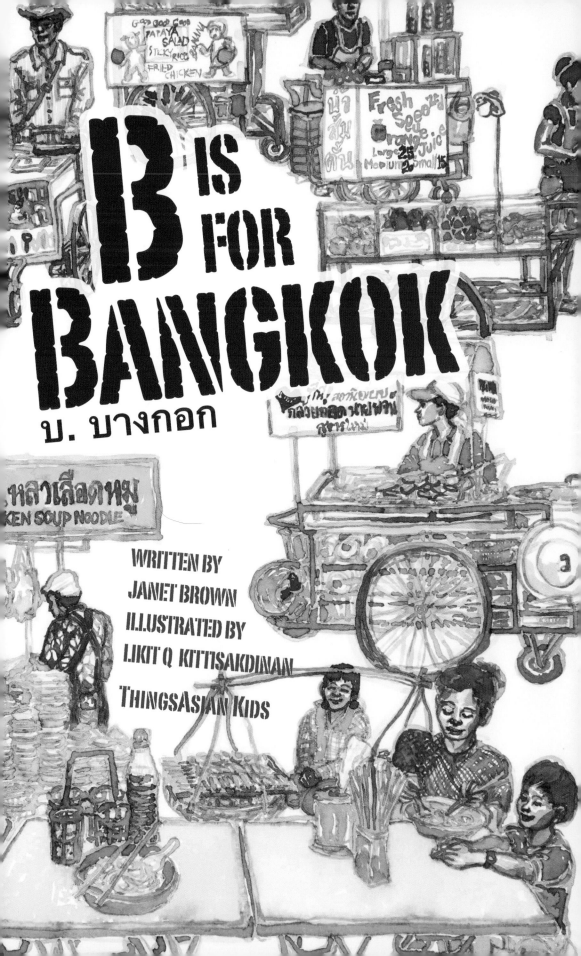

B IS FOR BANGKOK

บ. บางกอก

WRITTEN BY
JANET BROWN
ILLUSTRATED BY
LIKIT Q KITTISAKDINAN

THINGSASIAN KIDS

B is for Bangkok
Written by Janet Brown
Illustrated by Likit Q Kittisakdinan

Copyright ©2011 ThingsAsian Press

Edited by Janet Brown
Thai translation by Sirikul Saiseubyat Fong
Cover and Book Design by Janet McKelpin

For information regarding permissions, write to:
ThingsAsian Press
3230 Scott Street
San Francisco, California 94123 USA
info@thingsasianpress.com
www.thingsasianpress.com
thingsasiankids.thingsasian.com

Printed in Singapore
ISBN 13: 978-1-934159-26-2
ISBN 10: 1-934159-26-3

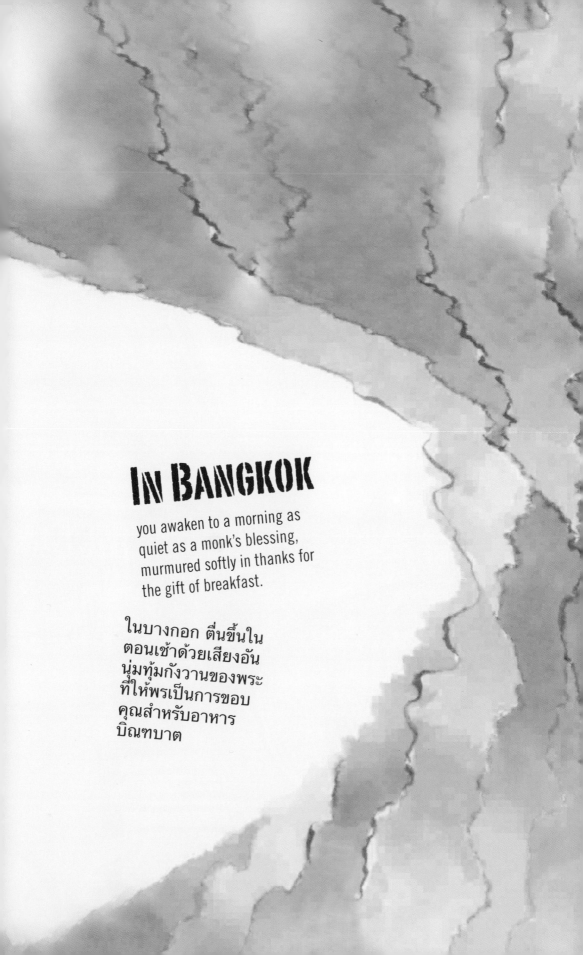

IN BANGKOK

you awaken to a morning as
quiet as a monk's blessing,
murmured softly in thanks for
the gift of breakfast.

ในบางกอก ตื่นขึ้นใน
ตอนเช้าด้วยเสียงอัน
นุ่มทุ้มกังวานของพระ
ที่ให้พรเป็นการขอบ
คุณสำหรับอาหาร
บิณฑบาต

To Work,
to School.—

are you one of the thousands of people who crowd on buses, subways, or trains that whisk you through the sky?

ไปทำงาน ไปโรงเรียน
คุณอาจเป็นหนึ่งในคนจำนวนนับพัน
ที่ต้องเบียดเสียดในรถประจำทาง
รถใต้ดินหรือรถไฟที่แล่นขนานท้องฟ้า

OR DO YOU

go to school on a boat

หรืออาจจะ ไปโรงเรียนทางเรือ

LEAVING

your house on a canal

ออกจากบ้าน ไปตามลำคลอง

TO TRAVEL

ALONG

the river under bridges
old and new?

ท่องเที่ยวไป ตามแม่น้ำ
ใต้สะพานทั้งเก่าและใหม่

OR MAYBE

YOU RIDE

a train that brings
you to a beautiful
Bangkok station
(Hualampong
Station)

หรือเลือกที่จะ
นั่งรถไฟ ที่พาคุณไป
สู่สถานีรถไฟที่
สวยงามของบางกอก
(หัวลำโพง)

JUST DON'T
TAKE A TAXI
unless you like
getting stuck in
a traffic jam!

อย่านั่งรถแท็กซี่
ยกเว้นแต่จะชื่นชอบ
การจราจรที่
ติดขัด

MANY TAXIS

are decorated with flowers and Buddha images for good luck—but that doesn't keep them from standing still for hours.

รถแท็กซี่มากมาย
ตกแต่งด้วยดอกไม้ต่าง ๆ
และพระพุทธรูป เพื่อสิริมงคล
แต่ไม่อาจช่วยให้รถเคลื่อน
ไหวได้นานนับชั่วโมง

POLICEMEN

TRY TO

keep cars moving—
some of them even
dance as they signal
to the traffic!

ความพยายามของตำรวจ
ที่จะให้รถเคลื่อนไหว
ตำรวจบางนายใช้ท่ารำ
พร้อมกับให้สัญญาณจราจร

IN A HURRY?
BREAKFAST
waits for you on the street—
fruit, fried bananas, little
coconut-milk cakes.

ในยามเร่งรีบ
อาหารเช้ารอคุณอยู่ตามถนน
ผลไม้กล้วยทอด ขนมแป้งจี่

IF YOU

CAN'T FINISH

your breakfast, the street's dogs and cats
will be happy to help you.

ถ้าคุณรับประทานอาหารเช้าไม่หมด
หมาและแมวข้างถนนเต็มใจจะช่วยเหลือ

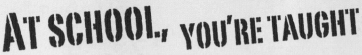

AT SCHOOL, YOU'RE TAUGHT

to dance like this, your
fingers learning to bend like
melting chocolate bars.

ที่โรงเรียน มีสอนรำ - นิ้วมือถูกดัด
ให้โค้งได้เหมือนความอ่อนของ
ช็อกโกแล็ต

MAYBE
YOU'LL PLAY

takraw at recess—don't touch the ball
with your hands!

บางทีคุณอาจจะเล่น ตะกร้อในเวลาพัก
ห้ามใช้มือจับลูกตะกร้อ

In November,
Your Teacher
Shows You

how to make floats covered with flowers and candles and sticks of incense to put in the river at night on a special day called *Loy Krathong*.

ในเดือนพฤศจิกายน คุณครู
แสดงวิธีทำกระทงด้วย
ดอกไม้และธูปเทียน
เพื่อลอยในแม่น้ำ ตอน
กลางคืนของวันสำคัญที่
เรียกว่า "ลอยกระทง"

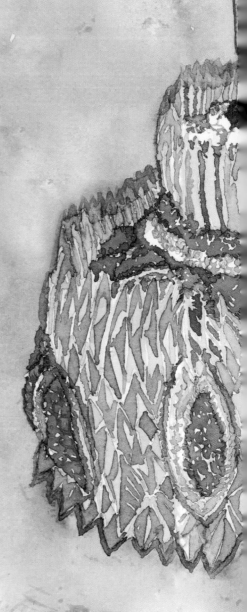

ON YOUR WAY

back home from school,
you can buy flowers.

ตามทาง กลับบ้านจากโรงเรียน
คุณสามารถซื้อดอกไม้

AND
FRUIT
และผลไม้

TO BRING HOME

for the spirit house that protects everyone in your home.

นำกลับบ้าน เพื่อถวายแก่
ศาลพระภูมิที่คุ้มครอง
ทุก ๆ คนในบ้าน

THIS IS A
SACRED TREE

that people wrap with colorful scarves—you can give it some of your flowers. (Bodhi tree)

นี้คือต้นไม้ศักดิ์สิทธิ์
ที่ผู้คนนำผ้าหลากสีมาผูก
คุณสามารถนำดอกไม้มาถวาย
(ต้นโพธิ์)

WANT AN AFTER-SCHOOL SNACK?

How about some stinky, delicious durian?

หากต้องการของว่าง
หลังโรงเรียนเลิก
ทุเรียน ที่มีกลิ่นฉุน
แต่รสชาติอร่อย
ลองไหม

IF IT ISN'T
A SCHOOL DAY,
you can play in Lumpini Park.

แต่ถ้าเป็นวันหยุด เด็ก ๆ
สามารถเล่นในสวนลุมพินี

**OR
GO TO**

Chatuchak Park's weekend market.

หรือจะไป
ตลาดนัดสวนจตุจักร
ในวันเสาร์ – อาทิตย์

A THAI MASSAGE

will loosen you up.

นวดไทยแผนโบราณ
ช่วยผ่อนคลาย

Lunch at a fancy hotel is a special treat and the receptionist will greet you in a special way,

"SA WAT DEE KAH."

อาหารกลางวัน
ในโรงแรมหรู ด้วยการ
ต้อนรับและนอบน้อม
ตามแบบพิเศษ
"สวัสดีค่ะ"

AFTER LUNCH,

it's fun to walk around the city.

หลังอาหารกลางวัน เพื่อความเพลิดเพลิน
ด้วยการเดินเล่นรอบ ๆ เมือง

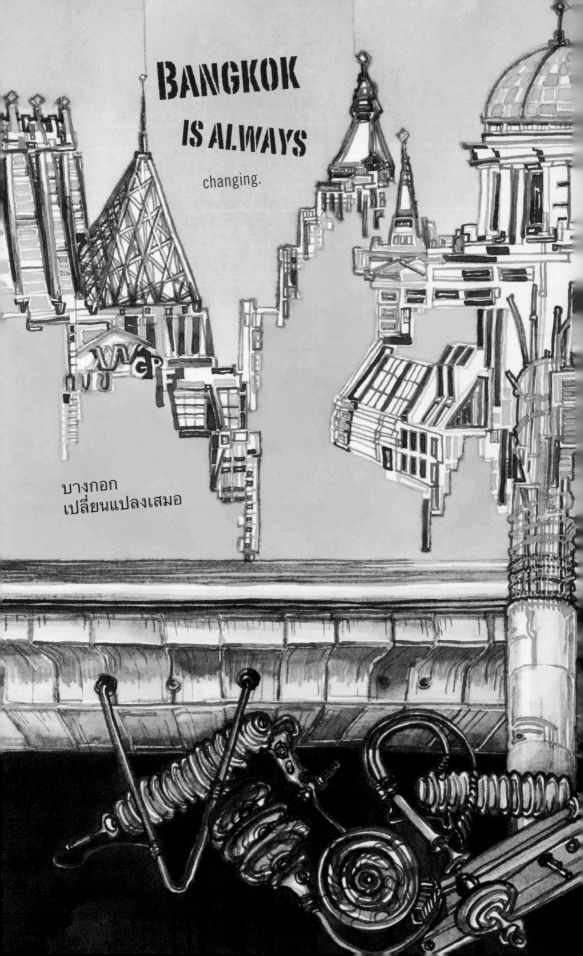

These CONSTRUCTION WORKERS transform the city, working all day and sometimes all night too.

คนงาน ก่อสร้างเมือง ทำงานตลอด ทั้งวันและบางทีตลอดทั้งคืน

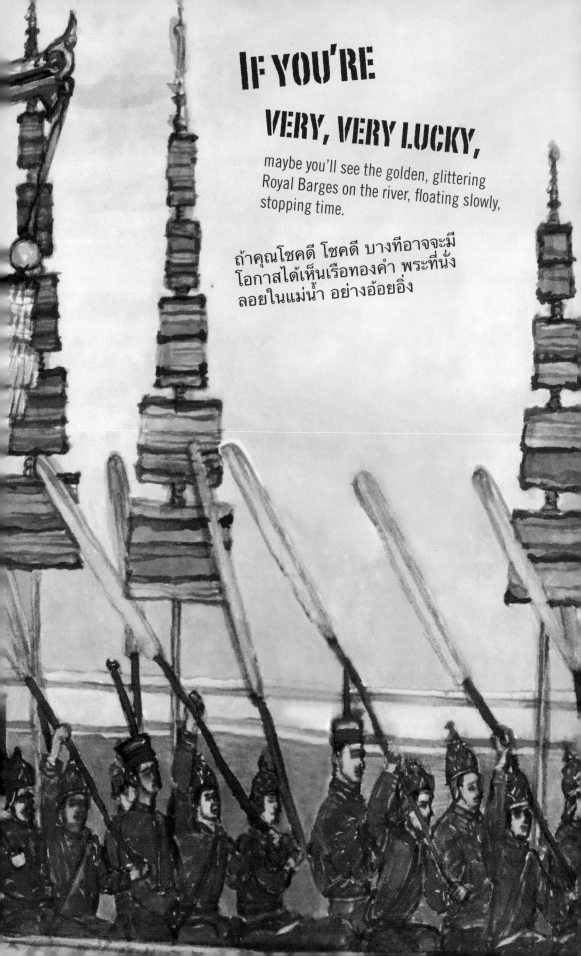

If you're
very, very lucky,

maybe you'll see the golden, glittering Royal Barges on the river, floating slowly, stopping time.

ถ้าคุณโชคดี โชคดี บางทีอาจจะมี
โอกาสได้เห็นเรือทองคำ พระที่นั่ง
ลอยในแม่น้ำ อย่างอ้อยอิ่ง

GET LOST IN CHINATOWN

and you're sure to find your supper!

หลงทาง ในเยาวราช (ไชน่าทาวน์)

และแน่นอนที่สุดที่คุณสามารถ
จะหาอาหารค่ำรับประทานได้

At the end
of every day,

Bangkok becomes
a garden of
brilliant,
colored lights.

ท้ายที่สุดของทุก ๆ วัน บางกอกกลายเป็น
สวนที่สว่างไสวไปด้วยแสงสีของไฟ

AND GECKOS
COME OUT TO PLAY,
watching over the city while you sleep.

และจิ้งจกออกมาเล่น
เฝ้ามองไปรอบ ๆ เมือง
ยามคุณหลับใหล

MORNING BLESSINGS

Thailand's capital city has the longest name of any city in the world (it's in the Guiness Book of World Records; you can look it up) and it has two nicknames. Thai people call it *Krung Thep (Kroong Tep)* and foreigners call it Bangkok. In the early morning all over the city, monks walk through the streets to receive the gift of food. They are not begging; they are giving people the opportunity to do a good deed.

SKY TRAIN BTS

In Bangkok, a train sweeps over the city on elevated tracks, carrying people past streets jammed with cars, trucks, motorcycles, buses and three-wheeled, covered vehicles called *tuktuks*.

RIVER TRAFFIC

River boats are a quick and cheap way to get through traffic.

LIFE AT THE CANAL

Across the *Chao Phraya* River that flows through Bangkok is a place called *Thonburi* where many people still live in old-fashioned houses built along the banks of canals.

HUALAMPHONG STATION
Bangkok's Hualamphong Station is where trains leave for every spot in the Kingdom. It's also the last stop for the city's subway.

COLORFUL TAXIS
Taxis in Bangkok come in many different colors— how many can you spot in this picture?

SUPERSTITIOUS TAXI-DRIVER
The dashboards of taxis hold little statues of the Buddha, garlands of flowers, and small clay tablets called amulets that bring good luck.

CATS & DOGS
Don't pet the animals you see on the street—most of them are afraid of people and some may bite.

STREET VENDORS
Food carts are everywhere in Bangkok— some have hot charcoal stoves on them so be careful not to bump into them as you walk down the street.

TAKRAW DYNAMIC
Takraw is played with a small rattan ball that is kept in the air with heads, feet, elbows—but not with hands.

MYTHICAL DANCE
Traditional Thai dance involves moving the hands in ways that seem impossible to people who haven't learned this in school.

LOY KRATONG
Loy Krathong is a special day when people make—or buy—little vessels called *krathong* that are traditionally made from a piece of a trunk from a banana tree and are floated at night down a river, carrying dreams and wishes with them.

CHILDREN & FLOWERS
Children often help their parents by selling flowers.

BRIDGES IN BANGKOK
There's a bridge built for every king who has ruled over Bangkok.

FRESH FRUIT
Fresh fruit is sold everywhere in the city, and is often dipped into a mixture of sugar and chili powder.

BODHI TREE
The Lord Buddha gained his wisdom when he sat under a bodhi tree, so Buddhists all over the world believe this tree is sacred.

SPIRITUAL HOUSE
Almost every yard in Bangkok has a little house on a pedestal for the spirits of trees and other things that were displaced when a house was built for people to live in. The spirits often are given little presents of flower garlands and sometimes bananas or oranges.

DURIAN
Durian is covered with sharp spikes and smells awful—but it tastes so good! It grows in orchards near Bangkok.

CHATUCHAK
Chatuchak Park is at the end of the city and has one of the biggest markets in the world where you can buy almost anything you want.

LUMPINI PARK
Lumpini Park is a big, beautiful green space in the middle of the city.

THAI MASSAGE
Thai massage is an ancient art that can cure almost any pain and is very relaxing.

CHINATOWN

Bangkok's Chinatown is one of the oldest parts of the city. Its narrow winding lanes are filled with wonderful places to eat.

ROYAL BARGES

Before there were cars in Thailand, the King and his family traveled on golden boats that were shaped like dragons. For special occasions these Royal Barges float down the river in a procession that seems as though it will never end.

GECKOS

Geckos have sticky feet that let them run up walls and cling upside down to ceilings as they catch mosquitoes for supper.

SAWAT DEE

Thai people wai instead of shaking hands, bending their heads as they raise their hands in a gesture like a prayer. Instead of saying hello they say "Sawat dee," and then ka if they are girls and women and khrup if they are boys and men.

Map of Thailand

กรุงเทพฯ
Bangkok
*

Q LIKIT

Artist, photographer and architect Q Likit was born and raised in Bangkok and loves to share his city with people who long to know it as he does. Educated at Harvard University's Graduate School of Design with a master degree in architecture, Q has lived and worked in New York, San Francisco, and Boston. An enthusiastic traveler, Q eagerly explores different corners of the world but he's always hungry to return to his home in downtown Bangkok, where he's a regular customer at the best food stalls and the finest restaurants in the city.

จิตรกร, ช่างภาพ และสถาปนิก คิว ลิขิต เกิดและโตที่กรุงเทพฯ และอยากแบ่งปัน ความรู้สึกให้กับคนที่มีความต้องการอยาก จะรู้จักกรุงเทพฯ เหมือนที่เขาได้สัมผัส การศึกษาจบปริญญาโท ด้านสถาปัตยกรรม จากมหาวิทยาลัย ฮาเวิร์ด คิวอาศัยและทำ งานอยู่ที่เมืองนิวยอร์ก ซานฟรานซิสโก และบอสตัน, คิว, นักท่องเที่ยวมืออาชีพ, ท่องเที่ยวไปทุกซอกทุกมุมของโลก แต่เขา มีความต้องการอย่างมากที่จะกลับมายัง บ้านเกิดในใจกลางเมืองของกรุงเทพฯ ที่เขา คุ้นเคยกับอาหารเลิศรสของร้านข้างทาง และร้านอาหารสุดหรูในเมือง...